Glint

Glint

LOIS PARKER EDSTROM

MoonPath Press

Copyright © 2019 Lois Parker Edstrom

All rights reserved. No part of this publication may be reproduced, distributed, or transmitted in any form or by any means whatsoever without written permission from the publisher, except in the case of brief excerpts for critical reviews and articles. All inquiries should be addressed to MoonPath Press.

Poetry
ISBN 978-1-936657-43-8

Cover photo "Tide Pool Treasures" © by Ronda Broatch
For more from this artist, go to:
https://fineartamerica.com/profiles/ronda-broatch.html

Author photo by Mel Edstrom

Book design by Tonya Namura using Minion Pro, Bilbo Swash, and Futura Condensed

MoonPath Press is dedicated to publishing the finest poets living in the U.S. Pacific Northwest.

MoonPath Press
PO Box 445
Tillamook, OR 97141

MoonPathPress@gmail.com

http://MoonPathPress.com

ACKNOWLEDGMENTS

Grateful acknowledgment is made to the editors of the following publications in which these poems first appeared.

"Canine Grace," *The Log*, 2018

"Engagement," read at Spokane Wedding, 2018

"Fragile Beauty," *Barnstorming*, 2018

"In a German Forest," Outrider Press anthology, *Music in the Air*, 2013

"Last Days," read at Memorial Service, 2016; World Enough Writer's anthology, *Coffee Poems*, 2019

"My Friend Alice," read at Memorial Service and published, 2017

"Rebecca Ebey," *Washington 129 Project*, 2018, Digital Edition

"Small Town Coffee Shop," World Enough Writer's anthology, *Coffee Poems*, 2019

"The Theory of Everything," *Poems in the Waiting Room*, 2019

"Wolf Moon," Outrider Press anthology, *The Moon*, 2017

My thanks to Teresa Wiley for providing a peaceful mountain retreat where quietness is the patron of poems, for proofreading the manuscript, and for the gift of laughter.

Thanks to Diane Stone and Sheryl Clough for their skillful reading, insightful suggestions, and unfailing friendship.

As always, thanks to Lorraine Healy who sent me on a blissful poetic journey.

I'm grateful to Evan Edstrom for the very best technical support.

I've been fortunate to work with a generous and gifted editor, Lana Ayers. Thank you, Lana. Thanks also to Tonya Namura for skillful design work.

As always, love in abundance and thanks to my family and dear friends who enrich my life beyond measure.

For My Sister, Claudia

TABLE OF CONTENTS

Part 1

THE THEORY OF EVERYTHING	5
THE HOME STRETCH	6
FLIGHT PATH	8
MIRABILIA	9
REBECCA EBEY	10
BRUISER	12
WAITING FOR THE FERRY	13
LOW BLOW TO THE EGO	14
CANINE GRACE	15
RIPE SEASON	16
THE OLD SHED	17
FIRST BITE	18
THE EDGE	19
SEASON OF THE HERON	20
NOVEMBER	22
GEORGE	23
FOG	24
THEOLOGY OF TREES	25

Part 2

WOLF MOON	29
A QUIET KINDNESS	30
LETTER TO EMILY STELLA GRACE	31
A SMALL POEM ABOUT SOMETHING BIG	32
ALL OF IT	33

UNASKED QUESTIONS	34
CADENCE	36
ODE TO OLD AGE	37
THE QUIET ONE	38
LAST DAYS	39
THE SMALLEST THINGS	41
MY FRIEND ALICE	42
DE PROFUNDIS	43
SMALL TOWN COFFEE HOUSE	44
IMPROVISATION	45
FAMILY PORTRAIT	46
STRANGE BEDFELLOWS	47
OUTSIDE LOOKING IN	48
SYMPHONY OF SILENCE	49
IN A GERMAN FOREST	50
PRAYER	51
BROKENNESS	52
FRAGILE BEAUTY	53
THE CLERIC OF SPRING	54

Part 3

KISSING THE BLARNEY STONE	57
ST. MARY'S AUTUMN RUMMAGE SALE	58
ANATOMICAL ODDITIES	59
FREE RANGE KID	60
AFTER DISASTROUS CHILDHOOD RECITALS	61
BAD MAMA	62

FEELING LOW	64
THE GARDENERS	65
RAYA	66
CURIOUS JOURNEYS	67
CHANGING TIMES	68
CONFESSIONS OF A YEASAYER	69
SMALL TOWN SATURDAY NIGHT	70
PORCINE DREAMS	71
SEPTEMBER	72
THE TIME BETWEEN	73
OCTOBER	74
THE FAR EDGE OF LONGING	75
ENGAGEMENT	76
NOTE TO MYSELF	77
NEBULOSITY	78
About the Author	79

Glint

Part 1

Take time to see the quiet miracles that seek no attention.
—John O'Donohue

THE THEORY OF EVERYTHING

If everything's connected, I want to be

the green of a leopard's eye. I want to be

a snowflake, among other snowflakes,

each unique, poised on the bareness

of a winter branch. I want to be

the glint of light on a summer wave,

a speck of salt in a tear of joy,

the giggle of a small boy playing

in a puddle of mud. I want to be

the space between notes in the intermezzo

of Mascagni's opera, the fragrance

of lilac in the spring.

If everything's connected, I want to be

a striation of muscle in your beating heart.

THE HOME STRETCH

It has taken a long time to build our house.
Years of labor, every nail and shingle

and brick placed by my husband's hand or mine.
When will you be finished? the uninitiated ask.

Look beyond a thousand lengths of forest,
the burnished sheen of copper, fields of tile

and glass, beyond a wall of stone.
It will be done when it is done.

It is almost finished now. The neighbors
have come for a party. We extend

our large antique table to accommodate
them, the table laden with food and flowers

gathered from our gardens. Books fill the shelves
in our library, and from two chairs in the bay alcove

on the second floor we note how light dances
on Crockett Lake, how clouds part,

like opening night at the opera, to reveal
the luminary of the Pacific Northwest: Mount Rainier.

Tugs pulling barges, cruise ships, sailboats,
cargo vessels, and an occasional submarine

pass through Admiralty Inlet heading
for the Strait of Juan de Fuca and the Pacific Ocean.

Deer come to our back door, look in the window,
ask for apples. Feral cats drink our milk.

We look skyward for aerial entertainment.
Herons, crows, hawks, owls, eagles

and the seasonal excitement of wild geese,
their flight an inspiration of purpose and intent.

My husband and I are also creatures of purpose.
We have a little trim work to finish.

Nail holes to fill, touch-up painting here and there.
How long has it been? acquaintances ask.

And we say, *Too long, but not long enough.*

FLIGHT PATH

I hear them before I see them,
raucous excitement coming from the north

and I run out to witness dark approaching clouds
that splinter into familiar aerodynamic chevrons:

the wild geese, waves and waves of them,
cresting over the house toward the lake at dusk.

Is it their fidelity to the season that lifts us up
to meet them, as if we are being birthed

into new expectations? Maybe we don't need to know
of the magnetic pull that directs them toward the poles

or the landmarks they remember
from earlier journeys. I like the mystery;

stars beginning to prick the deep of night,
winged silhouettes against the full moon.

MIRABILIA

A question no one can seem to answer.
What's to be done with beauty?

A sweep of melody that lifts to the crest
of weeping. The colors of water

swirling below Deception Pass Bridge,
hues so pure yet elusive.

The light and shine of satin in a Singer Sargent
painting—too much to take in; it spills

from a vessel of gratitude. Sunlight on the inlet
as it flashes toward night

like a mythological sequined fish breaking
waves into strands of silver and gold.

The cinnamon, nutmeg, and clove fragrance
of apple butter simmering all day in a heavy pot.

A quivering dewdrop on the cusp of autumn
that clings to the tatting of a spider's web.

What's to be done? I cannot hold these things
nor let them go.

REBECCA EBEY
1822–1853, Whidbey Island

Her house stood against the evergreens
at the edge of the prairie where farmland
partners with the sea.

It is as if she drifts in the fog that pockets
the fields of the land claim; her loneliness a sigh
in the wind that sweeps across Perego's Bluff

where she walked, scanning the horizon
for incoming vessels: the bright sails,
the returning tide a certain comfort.

Mother of two small boys, Mr. Ebey often
away on territorial business, she longed
for family left behind in Missouri;

illness and isolation her constant companions.
On a clear day her gaze rose to the *snow mountains:*
Mt. Baker, Mt. Rainier, and the Olympics,

those silent peaks that somehow steadied her.
Less than two years after she stepped
onto the island where *all around seems*

beautifully adorned in quiet serenity,
four months after the birth of a daughter,

she closed her eyes for the last time,
her funeral the first among the settlers
who came ashore aspiring to new beginnings.

Alone in a garden shadowed with grief
Mr. Ebey found a tendril of comfort
in the appearance of a dove that lingered

near him and memories folded back
upon themselves, two lives pleated together
when hope was young.

*Note: Italicized quotes come from a diary in which both
Isaac and Rebecca Ebey recorded observations and events.*

BRUISER

No one seems to know how he got here, the massive bull elk
with a rack of antlers the size of Mount Baker.

He showed up at Strawberry Point on the north end
of Whidbey Island.

We have not had elk on the island for at least
one hundred years.

Some speculate he swam across Skagit Bay
from the mainland

or separated from the North Cascade herd and walked
across Deception Pass Bridge.

He has been here four years now and he is lonely.
We hear him bugling in the night.

Never aggressive, he has a lot of untamed energy
during the post-rut season.

He plays kick the can with a five-gallon bucket,
overturns yard chairs, rakes his antlers through

Christmas lights and dents barbeque grills.
Lawn ornaments are especially vulnerable.

Neighbors, protect your gnomes.

WAITING FOR THE FERRY

He sits, leaning forward on his cane,
face as open and friendly as a daisy.

A young woman wrestles a large
orange leather bag through the turnstile,

finds a seat beside him. *Going to stay
overnight?* he asks, pointing toward

the bag. *Oh, no. This is what I need
for the day.*

I can't see whether he has a wallet
in his back pocket, but it's obvious

he travels light; has everything
he needs.

LOW BLOW TO THE EGO

My husband and son are kind, sensitive men.
I don't understand how this happened:

We return to our car after walking off the ferry
following a trip to Port Townsend.

I choose the back seat, but find the back door locked.
While tapping on the window, trying to get their
    attention,

they take off. I'm left standing in the parking space
four miles from home.

Surely one of those thoughtful men will notice
I'm not in the car.

Didn't happen that way. They drove home, only then,
surprised I didn't respond when they spoke to me.

Where's your mother?
I don't know. Maybe she is getting the mail.
I didn't stop there.

I was told my husband leaned over the seat to check
the floor as if I was somehow hidden from view.

Driving back to pick me up, my son, who has always
admired his father said, *I'm glad I'm not you.*

CANINE GRACE

Donnie attends church every Sunday morning.
He guides Chuck to a back pew,
lies down at his long-time companion's feet.
Sunlight through stained glass windows
gilds his blond fur with rainbows.
He enters into an hour of silence,
his own realm of meditation,
or sleep. Just before the benediction
Donnie stands, shakes his harness,
his unique practice in the ringing of bells.
His expression is hopeful
as the two of them head toward
the fellowship hall. Will there be
a cookie, or perhaps a bit of left-over
communion bread?

RIPE SEASON

Picking blueberries and I think
there is a poem here, but I can't find it.
The sun is warm. I shade my eyes, peer
through foliage dense and summer green.

Fat blueberries hang in tight clusters.
Their wild beauty springs from high
mountain meadows; the berries,
now cultivated in my garden,
even when baked into pancakes, muffins,
and pies, cannot be tamed. They burst,
spilling unrestrained flavor upon the tongue.

The green ones, tight and unyielding,
lack sweetness and I ponder this, pledging
to loosen my grip on preconceived notions.

My pail fills as ripe blueberries,
like miniature moons the color of twilight,
fall into my palm.

THE OLD SHED
Wind Dancer Lane, Whidbey Island

Nature waits to regain what it loves, its overtures endless.
It wraps itself around the old shed, ivy clambering
to the peak, wild cherry leaning over the ridge.

A climbing rose scales one wall, and bearded iris
clump around foundation stones
edging deeper into the earth.

Like a prodigal child, the building has squandered
its charms on those who framed it, raised it
from the trunks of fir and hemlock.

Stones lifted from earth's belly,
fragrant shingles borrowed from nature's salon.
The downward slope of roof has been there all along.

Now it tilts inward the way a dying person gathers
memories, a careful packing—tucking and folding
simple moments into a satchel of inner life.

It is quiet now, a boarded-up door.
No shafts of light to ignite dust motes
as they fall.

Nature waits to claim what it loves,
a smooth turning from one season to the next,
the mysterious certainty of change.

FIRST BITE
They wait like lowered gates while the mystery rolls past.
—Tomas Transtromer

Something intriguing about an old
homestead orchard, the farmhouse
and outbuildings long gone, yet
the trees hold vigil to time

planted by someone
who had foresight to know,
one hundred years later,
these trees would still need air
and light, space to shape
arabesques against the sky.

Massive trees bent, gnarled
and swathed in lichen,
they stand as fairy tale giants
bearing gifts—King apples as large
as a human heart, tantalizingly
suspended beyond reach.

As with all things beyond
our knowing, it is there we find
our fascinations. First-bite-magic
you can only imagine. Blood-red
lips that press around the crunch
and sigh of an enchanted sleep.
First bite that sent us spinning
in sunlit meadows of choice;
careening through dim forests,
just at the edge
of what we cannot see.

THE EDGE

We walk by the edge of the sea trusting
it will honor its boundaries

and at the edge of happiness hoping
it has no boundaries.

Love, that fragile thing, even love
can teeter on the edge of hurt,

become more or less than we can fathom.
We live at the edge of time

measuring our days by the ordinary
and the extraordinary. The edge of surprise

that widens our eyes to what is given.
This morning I stand in sunlight, taken in

by the fragrance of the newly mown field,
the melodic notes of our porch chimes,

beyond the edge of contentment.

SEASON OF THE HERON

On this wind-swept part of the island
exposed on the prairie above Crockett Lake

our weathervane perches on the northern
most peak of the roof—a verdigris heron

graceful symbol of those elegant birds
that come into our fields when fierce storms

batter the bird sanctuary at the lake.
The wind becomes an unrelenting presence.

At first a puzzling hum, a catch in the air
that gathers force, bends the evergreens,

stirs up the sea, howls
like a child lost in the night.

We hear the weathervane turn
on its moorings in tandem with the wind

as a winter storm comes ashore,
thrashes through the starless night.

This morning one wing leaves the body,
flies into the garden, followed by a foot.

Now turned skyward, a vertical bearing,
its remaining wing broadside to the wind,

we witness the heron's stunning demise.
In a final approximation of presumed

flight the heron leaves its post
bumps once on the roof and flies

into the field where it lies
in crumpled submission.

NOVEMBER

November's leaves have slipped
their mooring. Now they belong
to the wind and rain and earth.

Once glowing among evergreens
like eyes of the wild, they collect
in sodden masses against curbs

and over the grates of storm drains.
There is nothing to recommend
them, their beauty sacrificed
to the work of the season.

The necessary letting go
of things past to herald
another cycle.

Now we look to the sculptural
shapes of unadorned trees
against a winter sky,

simplicity its own beauty.

GEORGE

We see him walking in our small town.
This dear old man who lost his wife.

Never chunky, he is thinner now,
as if grief consumes his calories.

He circles down to the cove, soldiers
up the hill to the library, past the hospital,

and three miles out to the cemetery
on the prairie.

He walks, head down, elbows out,
arms swinging, as if urgency

has promised to find some trace of her
if he is swift enough to catch up.

His breath comes fast, lingers
in the mist of a cold day.

They say exercise, fresh air helps,
but I wonder if he is clocking

the miles to his own departure.

FOG

There is something mysterious about fog.
It whispered to Sandburg as it crept into the harbor

on little cat feet. It settles over Admiralty Inlet,
a downy comforter of relief on a simmering summer day.

It moves in quickly, a cool mist that settles lightly
on our faces and arms as we trudge up the hill

toward home. Then the stillness, how it tamps down
sound, reminding us to honor silence and drift

through an inner landscape of ideas,
enter into the ethereal magic of another world,

as if we were birds soaring in clouds
that have come down to enfold us,

quieting the minor furies we create.

THEOLOGY OF TREES

We have to believe one can change,
yet so much uncertainty. The bondage
of primordial markers. Genetics
that allow movement, but mainly,
within a confined space. Habits
that seem as fixed as knots within a tree.

Even so, with time and proper conditions,
knots, those rough-edged whorls, scab over
as lower branches atrophy, fall away,
and the tree continues to grow. Scars remain
within the tree, but new growth moves
outward, becomes fine-grained, flawless.

Today the wind changes direction
as if it can't make up its mind and the lake,
full of deep and unseen things, reflects the sky.

Part 2

To walk quietly until the miracle in everything speaks is poetry enough, whether we write it down or not.

—Mark Nepo

WOLF MOON

The January moon is ripe. It spills its light
into the dark night, an extrovert needing to be
the center of attention. There is a reason
wolves howl when the moon reveals the fullness
of itself, and although I haven't done so,
I've felt the urge—a longing so ancient and wild
as if in a time past we came from an enchanted place,
a place so beautiful we want only to return.

Now the moon casts its cold white light
onto everything—the fields glitter and the lake
gives itself up to receive the radiance
of that dominating presence.

We may lose ourselves in brilliance,
an attraction that smolders, just waiting to be lit.
No secrets, no dark and quiet corners.
The moon demands clarity.

Come into the light.

A QUIET KINDNESS

Spokane, a cold winter night. Eight of us
enjoying the warmth of a Chinese restaurant.
Good conversation and laughter, plates heaped
with Sesame Chicken, Ginger Chicken,
Pork Dumplings, Kung Pao Shrimp, Broccoli Beef,
arranged in the center of the table.

As we prepare to leave, I wonder why
my daughter-in-law asks for a take-home container
and a pair of chop sticks when we are headed for a concert.
Outside on the street, she walks back in the direction
from which we had come and hands the food
to a homeless man sitting on the sidewalk, hunched
against the cold.

He eagerly opens the container and begins eating.
I had also seen this man as we walked to the restaurant
and quickly forgot about him.

While it's good to live in the moment, claim the joy
and pleasure of light-hearted times, how easy to forget
those who live in the shadows and shade of need.

LETTER TO EMILY STELLA GRACE

Your parents taught you about respect,
about choice, and it seems you have an innate
understanding of kindness and grace.

Don't be afraid of happiness. It benefits everyone.
Don't be afraid of failure. It only means you get another
chance to try and it's not even failure unless
you fail to learn from it.

I've never believed that oft-repeated, supposedly freeing,
platitude, *you can be or do anything you want.*
You can't. We have unique talents. Know yourself
well enough to realize where your gifts are stockpiled.

You don't need to smite dragons or offer yourself
on the altar of achievements. Just be who you are.
Be willing to tell your story.

I like that you have the determination to figure it out
and the courage to take chances.
Breathe deeply, love deeply, and don't forget
to use sun screen.

A SMALL POEM ABOUT SOMETHING BIG

I've long thought it's all about light.
How it persists; creeps under closed doors,
rises each morning to defeat darkness.

It seeps from the full moon;
a silver drizzle across the face
of Crockett Lake

and is there in my beloved's eyes
at the beginning of each day,
a beacon that guides me to what is true.

Babies, those angels of light;
we are blinded by the flare
of their smiles, of who they are.

An irresistible light leads people
on a final journey and now scientists,
working with in vitro fertilization,

have seen microscopic sparks
of light at the exact moment
of conception.

ALL OF IT

Too much has been said of love and not enough.
How to speak of inner tides, light on a restless sea.

Fog, obscure and quiet, drifts in without warning
dampens the bell buoy's distant clanging.

We nibble at the edges of love's mystery
replete, yet forever starved.

We are like mariners without charts,
scribes without pens.

A moonflower blooms in darkness.
A dragonfly rests with open wings.

Shattered glass forms the mosaic's design
and swallows gather before parting.

All of it, all of it—salt and light.
Solving the mystery is as futile as trying

to steal a fingerprint.

UNASKED QUESTIONS

I wish I had known more about my father's life,
but I was young and full of myself.

I've been told he traveled to Alaska
when he was nineteen, worked in the gold fields.

Was he excited or fearful when he left his family home?
What did he learn from his adventures?

I was too young to remember him building our home
but stories accumulate over the years.

How he tore down an old house in our small town,
reclaimed lumber and bricks, straightened the nails,

laid a foundation, finding a way to provide a home
in the jaws of The Great Depression.

I wish I would have asked him how he found
his strength, how he persevered—life lessons

free for the taking. I've been told a mouse ran
up his pant leg while he worked, spawning

an ongoing phobia. He nailed metal can lids
over every knot hole in the house.

I wish we had talked about how you do your best
and learn how to live with what can't be fixed.

He gave family and friends nicknames as if by naming
the people close to him he brought them closer.

We could have talked about friendship. I saw how
he gathered friends; cared for those who needed help.

I think about how hard he worked owning a gas station,
tending our garden and orchard, providing for his family.

It was important to him that his children be well-dressed
and fitted with good shoes, but I know almost nothing

about his inner life. He seemed happy.
Was he?

Toward the end he told me his great satisfaction
was that all three of his children had college educations.

Did he miss having those same opportunities?
Would he have chosen a different life work?

I cared for him during the months he struggled
with terminal illness. They say pain is the price

you pay for having a heartbeat. I couldn't ask,
What is the hardest part of dying?

I couldn't answer him when he asked me, *How long?*

CADENCE

Rhythm is always on the move
and we are always chasing it

even though it fits itself nightly
through the moon's engagement ring,

spills onto the shores of our expectations,
cycles through the bodies of women

and soothes babies
with a rocker's squeak.

We are as greedy for the unchanging
measure of time as an infant for the nipple.

And what does it matter?
Would we increase or retard the tempo?

The pulse of nature saturates everything
and we breathe its harmonies,

a hamlet in our upturned soul.
Its allure the security

of the next predictable beat
or perhaps the silence between.

ODE TO OLD AGE
after a photograph by Emily Gibson

The over-ripe ear of corn still attached,
midwinter, to its spring-green stalk
may have surprised someone.

The husks, dry, grayed, and mottled with mold,
have been pulled away, the ear exposed,
the once tender kernels tough and wrinkled

and cracked. The delicate pale silk at the top
of the cob has blackened. Nostalgia
begs to remember the butter, the salt,

the picnics of an earlier season. Yet there is beauty
in the wizened features, the soft fading color,
the fierce resilience to survive the rain, the wind, and ice.

Now birds come. They have need of nourishment
as snow covers the gardens and fields and trees.
They partake and are filled.

THE QUIET ONE

Somehow, it is difficult to write about my mother.
Although she's been gone for many years
it is as if the closeness we shared
cannot be shared with others.

A patient, quiet woman, she never spanked
or uttered criticism. Do we ever know
how much we're loved?

On cold winter mornings she warmed my clothes
by the stove before helping me dress for school
and I remember a cabled sweater with pearl buttons
she knitted for me.

Her gentleness flowed to her grandchildren
and as they got older they teased her about how
she always ran to answer the phone on the first ring.

Hers was a subtle strength. In times of adversity she said,
You do what you have to do. As I left home, a reminder,
You are responsible for your own happiness.

That is all I can tell you, for now, about my mother.
What she gave me is like knowing when the tide goes out
it will always come back in.

LAST DAYS
in memory of Bebe

I could only think to give her bread.
What else to offer a woman

who has everything she needs
tucked into a valise of valor.

By her side, a good man who loves her
and two devoted dogs.

A hearth fire to settle by on chilly
autumn nights.

A bowl of heirloom tomatoes
fresh from the garden.

And those hens, *the girls*, that aerate
and operate the egg factory.

Once again to feel snowflakes
on her lashes at the cabin in Montana,

the warmth of morning coffee and a walk
in sunshine as bright as her smile.

So, I bring her something simple
from my hands to hers:

cardamom bread braided
with my esteem

and hot cross buns
just in time for Easter;

each bun risen and marked
with the sign of peace.

THE SMALLEST THINGS

He was a large quiet man, our uncle.
His mother died when he was a boy. He was raised
by a single father and two older brothers. So long
alone, they could barely remember the soothing simmer

of soup on the stove, the fragrance of flowers
on the table, the softness of a woman's touch.
He married our energetic, talkative aunt
after years of making his home in logging camps

and lonely sojourns in the mountains.
He had never held a baby. Who knows what undid him
when my infant sister was placed in his arms. The sweet
milky fragrance, the wide eyes, the delicate fingers

clutching his thumb. He was never quite the same,
so enchanted by this small creature. He held her for hours
as if his good fortune would come to an end
if he let go.

Not a shopper, he ventured to town, purchased
a little brown bear, tucked it next to her
in her basket as she slept. He was there for
her first steps, first words, and first boyfriend.

They remained close through the years, the bond
of a rough woodsman and a girl who grew, married
and had a daughter of her own. Then living in Hawaii,
my sister received a package addressed to the baby from
         Uncle Bud.

Nestled in tissue, a little brown bear.

MY FRIEND ALICE
for Karalee

My friend Alice, one of the wisest persons I know,
in early years devalued herself because she did not have
a college education.

We gave birth two weeks apart. My son lived.
Her son, her delicate blond boy, died before his first year.
We wondered how she could smile through

the waterfall of her tears. Then, an infant daughter
taken by a genetic disorder, a sweet angel child
she nursed for almost a year.

Our conversations went deep into the loam
of loss, how she tilled the soil of her grief
to find a field where something would take hold

and allow her to grow. Strength like that
doesn't sprout from text books and college degrees.
Now, many years later, thoughts swirling

in a whirlwind of dementia, she sometimes
recognizes her surviving daughter, sometimes not.
She understands this is someone dear, someone

who loves her and is loved, and she sends her off
with advice that has lodged in her mind like a shim
that balances and secures disparate parts:

Be good. Be safe. Be brave. Be happy.

DE PROFUNDIS

You may think, because I often smile,
my mouth is filled with denial, dark things
stuck between teeth so innocuous,
yet flagrant.

My life is not swallowed without tasting
bitter with the sweet, and what I know
of grief goes beyond the grindings
and grumble of complaint.

What remains is choice—to accept
what is with what is possible,
the two consumed together
and not without risk.

Don't we all court truth
in our own way? A carrot glows
beneath dark soil, its green tassel
only a hint of subterranean splendor.

To hope is like dancing against the wind,
a buoyant vulnerability, like ashes
that descend after fire.

SMALL TOWN COFFEE HOUSE

We don't know what to do.

We look at each other through a scrim of silence,

finger the thin hem of our understanding,

feel the frayed edge of heartbreak.

After the fog turned hard, after the shriek of steel,

the glitter of glass shards on the rain-slick road,

the hush of it everywhere.

How are we left with nothing but silence?

She didn't know when she left for work

that morning she would not arrive;

the young barista who always smiled

as she steamed our espressos

and the thing is

I didn't know her name.

IMPROVISATION

*...sometimes it is the artist's task to find out how much
music you can still make with what you have left.*
—Itzhak Perlman

It was reported he said this following a concert
at Lincoln Center after a string snapped on his violin.

He continued playing, at one with his music;
notes, like holy sparks, rose and spiraled

into the bodies and psyches of those in the audience.
The sweat, the tears amid cheers, the standing ovation.

Call it a gift of improvisation or simple perseverance.
And don't we all know the lesson here?

Aren't we all broken?

It doesn't matter if the story is true. Every day
is a growing season.

We can nourish ourselves on the richness of the quote.
Our task is to make music with what remains.

FAMILY PORTRAIT
for my friend

They are posed around a Christmas tree
and although I don't know them, they speak
to me through a sheen of silence.

I can barely hear the mother, hands folded on her lap
after all the chores are done. She whispers of devotion.
They all try in their own way, she says and I believe her.

Oldest sister, blossoming into the flush of independence,
sits to the left of a younger girl who kneels in the center
and that's where she stays, bringing them all together.

The young brother, head tilted to one side, seems wistful,
as if the burden of silence has not fully descended on him,
but he has glimpsed the large, immovable boulder that blocks

an icy river where the water must part, find particular
ways around; the father stands, separate from the family,
an arm resting on the top of a straight back chair.

Strands of tinsel fall from the tree like frozen tears
and beyond the window a pristine winter field blanketed
in snow gives no sign of what is hidden beneath.

STRANGE BEDFELLOWS

We don't belong to the night, nor it to us.
Its hospitality erratic, we enter through a curious
portal not knowing if we will descend into a deep
canyon of rest or a cave of winged terror.

Random events pull us pull us back
to forgotten pasts while our imaginations paint
astonishing scenes on the walls of our slumber.

Sleep, a drama like the half-darkened
face of Lady Macbeth, a mystery
that plays out again and again.

Frequent visitors, we willingly submit
to its paralyzing darkness, give ourselves
completely, with every assurance
we will return to the light.

OUTSIDE LOOKING IN
after a photograph in Iron Horse Literary Review

We see what we expect to see
in a forest of long-held beliefs, yet
reality may illuminate an unpredicted view.

The couple faces each other in a lighted
tent surrounded by darkness, cups tilted
toward one another.

We have no way of knowing if the wine
of desire, or a bitter concoction of resentment
fills those cups, their hopes held within the sturdy
rim of stoneware or fragile porcelain.

Alone, their isolation, like a venerated
sage, nurtures the truth.

And outside a fire burns unattended,
sparks spiraling into the night.

SYMPHONY OF SILENCE

A summer morning, driving down the island
to the coffee shop, sunlight filtering through alder leaves,

the bay a blue-green shimmer. We saw the flashing lights
of emergency vehicles clustered by the side of the road.

We saw the responders huddled together, an overturned
motorcycle in the ditch. The silent aid car

heading toward the hospital, too late for lights or siren.
Now silence beats its drum, a steady rhythm

that penetrates our understanding. Silence,
so often a comfort that travels inward

to the bright edge of creativity, now a deafening
syncopation that pounds in our ears, a crescendo of loss,

the finale of the morning's lament.

IN A GERMAN FOREST

Lately I am drawn to the silhouette of tree tops
in evening light, how a breeze stirs the leaves

exposing a silver underside and the trees sway
not exactly in rhythm, more a bending to the same

impulse, a slow tempo backlit by the moon,
seduction and fluidity of night.

Near Mittenwald trees make music.
Lumber buyers tap trunks to hear

the soul of a violin longing to sing,
or a Bosendorfer's sonorous, complex heart.

I hear the haunting movement
of Beethoven's *Pathetique*

pulse within the fibers and juice
of evergreen, course through branches

to the uplifted tips of its needles,
compressed into rings and rings of years.

PRAYER

Father, I am weary of the division in the world. The clang
of dissension, the clamor of estrangement and alienation.

A meadow filled with sunlight calls, and autumn light
softens the cottonwoods' golden furies as they shadow
the river. Doves released from the dovecote fly
their freedom. They turn in unison, an exquisite unfurling
that blesses sky.

I don't want to be one who turns away from ugliness
and the need that underlies it all, but the world
is splintered and what good comes of gathering kindling
only to build fires that burn cold?

Don't we all want to find our own understanding, come
to our own conclusions, and why do we think, for one
instant, that we could do that for another?

For now, I will seek the communion of flowers,
how the peony opens up to receive the light
and the lily-of-the-valley whispers, *You must also learn
to live in the shade.*

BROKENNESS

I am drawn to old abandoned houses. Perhaps
it's the ramshackle charm of their sway-back roofs,
moss staking a claim, and doors that hang askew
like sailors who have not yet found their sea legs.

I like the soft weathering of the siding, and vines
that reach up and out, clinging to any break
in the clapboards. I like the openings where glass
once framed the view to the outside.

I feel the urge to fix what's there, but that would be
like trying to fix a husband and removing all
those lovable imperfections.

I like thinking about the lives and passions
that simmered and flared inside those walls:
the knowing glances of a young couple over flickering
candlelight, a child reading in a plump feather bed,
an old man smoking a pipe in front of the fire,
a woman laboring in the birthing room.

Maybe I'm attracted to the stories of those bygone voices,
or the flaws; the brokenness of what sheltered them.

Maybe it is something about how the home holds on
even when it seems about to collapse.

FRAGILE BEAUTY
after a photograph by Emily Gibson

It's just a leaf. A damaged leaf at that,
clinging to a filbert tree ravaged by blight.
The leaf turns partially back upon itself,
riddled with holes, the traumatic result
of voracious insect appetites.

Damaged does not accurately describe
this leaf, the color of rich burgundy wine,
deep purple veins that branch to the tips
of its serrated edge. The holes open the leaf
to light and air, forming a filigree of nature,
an exquisite fragile beauty.

It makes me think of our own traumas,
how they open us, raw and hurting, humble us,
soften and expand us to the pain of others
and when we are most vulnerable we hold on,
weakened, but not necessarily damaged.
Perhaps it is then our scars become beautiful
and an inner loveliness shines through.

THE CLERIC OF SPRING

Green, its unending shades and permutations,
saturates the soul of spring with rich sincerity.

It elevates wild mustard that indoctrinates
a charm of goldfinch.

Lilacs burn their sweet incense in the midst
of green clouds. Our fields take on a quiet

reverence toward the lushness that comes
at winter's end; grassy reflections tint

the walls of our house. Peonies spread deep
green wings, pale pink buds crowning to the light.

The garden hails this season of ripeness with leafy
expectancy; asparagus spears burst

through the soil overnight and rhubarb meets my
enthusiasm for the season with foolish abundance.

How inscrutable this verdant tenderness,
a youthful domination of ancient renewal.

Part 3

A miracle is often the willingness to see the common in an uncommon way.

—Noah Benshea, *Jacob the Baker*

KISSING THE BLARNEY STONE

I was born with red hair. My dark-haired parents
climbed a ladder to the fourth rung before finding
an ancestor, a grandfather, with weak ties to Erik the Red.

Perhaps a Viking connection is why some redheads
are accused of having fiery tempers, although
the dragon seems only to ignite the fire in my brain
on the pyre of injustice.

My hair is described as *auburn*, a toned-down
version of red. These coppery tresses came with fair skin
and freckles across my nose; spots as unwelcome
as the plague.

My grandmother called them *angel kisses*,
said they would go away as I grew older
and they did.

Now I'm a grandmother and I find my hair
has not grayed, a peculiar result of being a redhead.

Identifying with my Scandinavian heritage
most of my life, DNA reveals my genetics
mainly island-hop in the U.K.

I should have known. I've never been partial
to lutefisk or careening down a mountain on skis.

Although only two percent of the world's population
has red hair, redheads top out in Ireland at ten percent.

I will gladly set aside the pickled herring
and aquavit for a good swig of Irish whiskey.

ST. MARY'S AUTUMN RUMMAGE SALE

This must be the light artists in the south of France
crave; how everything seems supercharged—
spun gold luster that gilds oaks and evergreens,
asters and hydrangeas, an intimacy of air and light.
I feel a quiet yet sudden change, as the tectonic plate
of autumn slides over a weary summer.

We walk past St. Mary's, see a throng of people
stretching from its doors out to the road.
A lot of people needing confession, my husband jokes.
A lot of sinning going on, a passerby responds.

We see the priest blessing the shoppers as they enter
the church. Outside the wind, that old prophet of autumn,
comes to claim its followers, leaves twirling, falling,
skittering along the road like brown-robed monks.

ANATOMICAL ODDITIES

Sitting in church I begin to study
ears. An irreverent preoccupation,
you say?

These odd, yet elegant flaps
like megaphones eavesdropping
rather than announcing.

Ridges of cartilage form large peninsulas
jutting out on disproportionate heads.

From the pulpit words crest
like waves, set tiny bones to chiming,

swirl down paired nautiluses,
cilia floating like seaweed,

the interior chambers waxed
as if prepared for a long sea voyage.

The sound bounces in the cavity
of these undersea caves

random sonar, uncertain images
that appear on the variable,

sometimes murky screens
of our brains.

FREE RANGE KID

When I was a kid, the sun assaulted my skin.
My body fought back with freckles.

My body didn't understand the need
for self-protection, how a baton, thrown high
into the air, would come down with my dreams
of being a frisky majorette and hit me in the teeth.

How riding a bike down a gravelly hill would end
in a wipe-out and holding a BB gun incorrectly
would result in a crushed finger.

Playing by the creek I rushed headlong into a patch
of stinging nettles while trying to get close to a dragonfly,
its wings shimmering in sunlight.

Fences were to keep the cows in, not me out.
I found out otherwise when I touched
the electric wire.

When I was a kid, before I could swim, I slid down
a water slide into the lake against the advice
of my parents and watched bubbles escape my nose
until someone pulled me out.

When you are the victim of a happy childhood
you don't think about being hurt.

AFTER DISASTROUS CHILDHOOD RECITALS

It is a nightmare.
I'm appearing with Tony Bennett,
playing the piano.
Haven't played for years and even then
not well.
The notes look like city lights.
I'm a country person.
Chords stacked next to one another
like skyscrapers—
how to make sense of that?
A confusing bluesy nightscape.
I noodle along, one note at a time
hoping no one will notice; I'm dreaming
of course.
He sings his heart out, carries us both.
The end of the song he sits down near me.
I confess I'm out of my league.
He agrees.
I could call my son, I say. *He's a professional
jazz guy.* *Please,* he says.

My son, who knows most tunes from first note
and needs no music, says he has a gig,
can't come until later. *Improvise*, he said.
So I did.
I wept.

BAD MAMA

It started before we had kids: newlyweds, small apartment,
small budget, first Christmas.

My husband came home carrying a little evergreen tree,
a box of dime store baubles, and one special,

more costly ornament. The appeal of this
tennis-ball-sized extravagance seemed to be

that it glowed in the dark. Its color was sickroom green,
embellished with hand-painted Pepto-Bismol roses.

I ascribed this choice to the premise that tastes
in a young adult male may not be fully developed.

After a few years our sons arrived, first one,
and three years later, another.

Following the example set by their father,
our sons chose the glow-in-the-dark ornament

as their favorite. Each year I tried, discreetly,
to hang the ornament in an inconspicuous place.

After lights out for the night, the boys snuck out of bed,
flashlight in hand and guided by its sulfurous glow,

moved the ornament to a place of prominence
front and center on the tree.

Families have various Christmas traditions.
This was ours.

Then one year, unpacking the holiday decorations, I found
the favored ornament shattered within its tissue wrapping.

I poured an eggnog with a splash of rum, cut a piece
of fruitcake, and had myself a little celebration.

The boys, then teenagers, looked at me with suspicion
when I told them about the breakage.

Call it good luck, call it fate or divine intervention, but now,
years later, when I remember, with fondness, that ugly

ornament, not one of those possibilities
relieves my nagging guilt.

FEELING LOW

Sometimes it feels good to feel bad

in a second-hand sort of way.

The slow footsteps, down-turned eyes, shoulders

slumped forward as your team leaves the field

after being severely trounced, last game of the season.

You can wallow in the misery and depression

of it all without really rolling in the mud—

give in to the wretchedness and when you feel

sufficiently low, think noble thoughts about

how character-building it is to accept defeat,

feel a bit self-righteous about your strength

in adverse circumstances, your ability to climb out

of the pit of despair, all the while giving thanks

for your comfortable, and for the moment,

fairly uncomplicated life.

THE GARDENERS

Two five-year-old imps, Emily and Nikko,
playing together at the family reunion

found dried poppy pods in a flower bed
at the end of the house. Busy, busy.

They sowed seeds far and wide, a heavy
concentration in the herb garden.

After thousands of the tiny black seeds
had been dispersed, they disclosed

what they had done. Call it a prank.
Call it an accident or the creativity

of children. The tall purple poppies
growing in a haphazard, yet elegant manner

are stunning. They grow in every flower bed,
sprout between stones in the pathway,

overtake the herbs. They are everywhere.
It's difficult now to find the oregano and thyme

when the sauce is bubbling, yet I can't contain
my joy as I think of the wanton exuberance,

the pleased expressions of those two gardeners.

RAYA

Reading, for her, is like an accelerant poured on flame.
She burns from the need to live with words.

A farm girl, she absorbs silence, hears the rhythms
of leaves, the music of raindrops, the churn of mycelium

working the earth. She wades in barnyard muck, carries
water, gathers eggs, feeds an eclectic mix of animals.

Unlike other kids who wait for the release of the latest
electronic gizmo, Raya yearns for a typewriter.

She has stories to tell—how her pig named Carol
ate the duck and chewed on the goat's ear.

How Carol had to go to market and any writer worth
a quilled pen knows one does not shy away from
    heartbreak.

How her bearded dragon, Smaug, is quite calm and sweet
unlike the fearsome dragon in *The Hobbit*.

How coyotes steal the turkeys and how the soft light
of dawn chimes like the ringing of a bell.

In this morning's mail I received a two-page letter,
single spaced, a story really...

Earlier in the week, recovered from the back of Raya's
great-grandmother's closet, neglected for thirty years,

a bright orange *Adler Contessa De Luxe* typewriter.

CURIOUS JOURNEYS

Lauren's beloved yellow lab died.
That very week—that very week,

a yellow lab showed up at her home,
a note tucked into its collar

that simply read *Lola*. How and why
the dog appeared there is a cold case mystery.

Lola, a sweet dog, has two issues.
She likes to run away and she loves bread.

Whatever Lola wants, Lola gets.
Any bread left untended is snatched

by Lola and scarfed to the last crumb.
An entire loaf of artisan bread, placed

to the back of the kitchen counter,
was found, claimed, and devoured.

More serious is Lola's other issue.
Lauren lives on a wooded hill

overlooking a beautiful Montana valley,
bears, cougars, and coyotes her close neighbors.

So, when Lola goes missing, Lauren goes
looking. On this particular day, Lauren is driving

the country roads looking for Lola when,
in the distance, she sees a dog coming toward her car

a loaf of bread in the dog's mouth.

CHANGING TIMES

Some days speak a language of contentment,
words of abundance, a song that pulses
in rhythm with my heart.

This summer morning, I need nothing more
than to walk to the market in sunlight, linger
near the peaches, nectarines, corn, baby lettuces,
arugula, and tomatoes mounded in outdoor bins.

The earnest young man arranging the fruit smiles,
as if the day is a gift wrapped in pleasure
and he the grateful recipient. I choose purple plums,
add a baguette, a sausage, a wedge of brie,
and chocolate for the picnic basket.

In the checkout line the woman behind me watches
as I write a check and I smile when I hear her say,
How quaint.

CONFESSIONS OF A YEASAYER

I feel as if I'm in the turbulence the ferry makes
when the prop reverses approaching the landing—
stirred up and restless, easily annoyed by almost
everyone and everything.

As a woman who normally sees the best in others,
elevates them to unattainable heights,
for the present, I'm glimpsing a few folks
in The Emperor's New Clothes, silly and unattractive.

It's not as if I'm on a lonely journey to nowhere,
but after a week of others piling on, all minor offenses,
I'm feeling the need for comfort and retreat.

I luxuriate in my favorite bookstore, there among the stacks
of poetry, shelves so high I need a stepstool to reach the top.
Tottering in the dusty loftiness of bliss, I sneeze.

From one stack over I hear, *Bless you*. I chuckle and say,
Thank you. Another sneeze, another *Bless you*. Wow,
twice blessed. Wonder if I could do this on demand.

I ponder the benefits, a book of Kumin essays in my hand.
Sometimes life is like a sneeze. The build-up, a minor
explosion, a sudden release of irritants, the return

to normal, and amazingly you breathe easily once again.

SMALL TOWN SATURDAY NIGHT

Hamburgers at our local eatery, a funky tavern that sports a moose head wearing a baseball cap, a toilet seat suspended from the ceiling, dusty photos of movie stars who ate here when *Practical Magic* was filmed in our town, and as you leave, a slanted wooden floor that makes you feel as if you have had more to drink than you have. Jaywalking across one of the two blocks of our main street, a SUV pulls up, a window opens, a blonde middle-aged woman, clearly in a heightened state of excitement, calls to us—*Chocolate Night in Coupeville* holds out a plastic container filled with Hersey's dark chocolate kisses. We each grab one, unwrap and eat without a moment of hesitation. *We may drop dead before we reach home*, my husband says, but hey, happiness is where you find it.

PORCINE DREAMS
after the phototgraph "Still Life, The Pig"
by Emily Gibson

Do we always want more than we need?
More time off. More travel.

Just one more piece of that tempting dark chocolate
filled with caramel, sprinkled with sea salt.

To hear that you're loved one more time
then again and again.

The best wine, the gourmet dinner, art that speaks
to the heart, must hang on our walls.

Our extravagant coffees and desires.
Another handbag. One more pair of shoes.

A fast, sleek car; a bigger boat, bigger waves,
greater danger.

The glory of praise. May it never stop.
We are such needy beggars.

How did the pig escape the barnyard? He is clean
and eats from a porcelain bowl rather than a trough.

Now he sleeps, face down in his empty bowl,
a slight smile tilting the corner of his mouth.

SEPTEMBER

One afternoon
summer measures its hem
and finds it has outgrown
its season, even now the shadows
falling toward autumn. It covers
its ears, refuses to hear
the skein of wild geese
unraveling in the sky
and how the wind churns
the willow's leaves, a faint
chatter like seeds shaken
in a dried-out gourd.
The air's moist expectancy
confirms what we know
to be true. The textures
and dimensions of change;
choice stitches us to the comfort
of the familiar, or snips
the threads that bind us
to what we have outgrown.

THE TIME BETWEEN

She is twelve gaining on thirteen
and moves with womanly grace.

I notice, when I tuck her into bed,
two fuzzy animals cozied by her pillow.

She wears a tattered bed jacket of pink nylon
sprigged with tiny blue flowers,

the neckline frayed, a bedraggled ribbon
dangling from one side.

I hug her and ask about the jacket.
It's my grandmother's, she says,

a grandmother I know died last summer.
She gathers the jacket to her nose and says,

It smells like her.

OCTOBER
Roslyn, Washington

There is such longing in the days
and nights of autumn, an obscure

pleasure just this side of sadness
as if the soul stretched to a thin

membrane admits luminous light
allows just the right amount

of darkness. Perhaps we need
disparity to learn grace. Stillness

of falling snow contradicts
the carnival of colors;

Aspen's golden coins jingling
in the mountains' pockets,

vine maples hawking their cinnabar
and copper wares. The season rotates

like a carousel; arrival spins
toward departure.

THE FAR EDGE OF LONGING

I keep going back to it. I don't know why
I'm so attracted to the photo of a dandelion
at its time of ripeness. Beyond the exquisite,
delicate beauty of the seed head,
there is something more.

Something about a seed partially detached
from the fragile orb, waiting for passage
to an unknown destination, the wind
an ancient conveyance.

Something about the slender shaft, the seed
poised at the tip like the point of a tiny arrow,
and the feathery fibers at the opposite end,
a miniature parachute set for descent.

Something about the potential of this humble
tuft of fluff uniquely prepared to be planted
in the place it belongs.

I imagine how it would feel to be lifted up,
carried away in the arms of the wind.
To drift in random flight, the allure
of not knowing how or when or where.

ENGAGEMENT
for Evan and Hannah, November 22, 2017

He chose a bride, a tender young woman
who said *yes* and happiness spilled out and over

and down upon us the way snowmelt pours
from the mountains on a warm spring day.

We come together for this journey and as we travel
through the mountains, these cathedrals of slanting light,

waterfalls spill down to meet the river on its way to the sea
where the blessings of abundance come together

and light bounces everywhere. It shatters rising mists
into rainbows and dances on the ripples of the river.

Happiness cannot be contained. It illuminates
two young faces.

It flows from a crystal spring deep within.
We drink and are filled.

NOTE TO MYSELF

We cherish celebratory events: weddings, births,
graduations, and promotions, but what of those fleeting,
yet exquisite, moments? Gentle snips of time that pass
unnoticed, squandered in pursuit of more exciting
possibilities or our unique forms of bliss.

Sometimes happiness sneaks up on you and you don't know
it's there until you sit in perfect silence: the sun warming
your skin, the sky feeding you its light, and waves
that come ashore lulling you into their soothing rhythm.

I will gather those moments like shells strewn
along the strand; an accumulation of evanescent memories
collected into a lifetime supply and, however fragile,
sort through their unique beauty, there for the taking.

Note to myself: Settle into yourself. Go beyond yourself.
Gather what you find, what's been given.

NEBULOSITY
Blue Moon, March 31, 2018

In the country, night becomes a deep well of darkness.
Coyotes howl success or disappointment; owls, those silent
missiles, aim at scuttering mice and rabbits
with deadly precision.

When my young grandson visits from the city, he says,
The stars are closer at your house, Nana, the Big Dipper tipped
to offer a cup of cool water, other stars winking, spilling
champagne, bubbles floating in a darkened sky.

This celebration of vastness, those distant counselors,
beacons, guiding us to mystery beyond ourselves.
They say love speaks with light. I will hold onto what I know,
mindful of what we can never know.

Tonight, a blue moon adds its radiance, overflows
across the lake. Like thirsty wanderers we drink the light
yet are never full.

About the Author

Lois Parker Edstrom, a retired nurse, is the author of four collections of poetry. *What Brings Us to Water* won the 2010 Poetica Publishing Chapbook Award. *What's To Be Done With Beauty* received the Creative Justice Award in 2012. *Night Beyond Black* was published by MoonPath Press in 2016. *Glint*, 2019, is her second full-length book.

She has received two Hackney National Literary Awards, the Outrider Press Grand Prize, and the Westmoreland Award. Her poems have appeared in literary journals such as *Clackamas Literary Review, Floating Bridge Review, Rock & Sling, Mobius,* and *Adanna*. In 2017, Edstrom's work received nominations for a Pushcart Prize and the Washington State Book Award.

Three of her poems have been read by Garrison Keillor on *The Writer's Almanac,* and one poem was featured in Ted Kooser's *American Life in Poetry*. In 2016 Edstrom's career in nursing and her poetic passion coalesced when her poem, *Choices We Make When We Are Too Young to Make Them*, appeared in *Poems in the Waiting Room*, a publication furnished to hospitals and to doctors' offices in New Zealand. Her poetry has been translated into braille, and has also been adapted to dance by the Bellingham Repertory Dance Company. The natural beauty of Whidbey Island, where she lives with her husband, inspires much of her work.

www.ingramcontent.com/pod-product-compliance
Lightning Source LLC
Chambersburg PA
CBHW020145130526
44591CB00030B/220